free YOUR SOUL

ALSO BY THE AUTHOR

THE HOME WITHIN - Haiku Poetry Prompts for Self-love Journal

LIFE ON FIRE JOURNAL - A daily prompt vision planner to thoughtfully plan, create your dream life, and fulfill your goals (pink, blue, and black color cover options)

Please scan the link above to view all the titles currently available by this author. Thank you.

THE PATH TO GREATER
PEACE, LOVE, JOY, HEALTH,
AND HARMONY

free YOUR SOUL

MURIEL OKUBO

DOCTOR OF ASIAN MEDICINE

Copyright @ 2024 by Muriel Okubo
Designed by Muriel Okubo
All Rights Reserved.

No part of this book may be reproduced, distributed, transmitted or amended in any form or by any means, including photocopying, recording, or other electronic or mechanical methods, without prior written permission of the publisher, except in the case of brief quotations embodied in reviews and specific other noncommercial uses permitted by copyright law. No graphics or images from this book may be copied or retransmitted without the Muriel Okubo's express written permission.

Hardcover ISBN: 978-1-0688444-0-9
Paperback ISBN: 978-1-0688339-3-9
EBOOK ISBN: 978-1-0688339-4-6

This book is dedicated to everyone on a journey to align with their inner heart and find the truth of their soul. Take all you need and leave all that you don't. Enjoy each poem with an open heart.

ACKNOWLEDGEMENT

To my Mom,

You are my best friend in the world. I live more courageously because you strengthen me whenever we speak, or meet. You ignite my soul with your voice, your kindness, your essence. You tell my soul what it needs to hear. I am your baby forever. I am blessed to know you and to have experienced life with you. You have pushed me when I didn't trust myself. I was able to bloom because you saw all I held within me before I could. Your authenticity has taught me the truth behind love. With elegance and grace, you have taught me that life is always better when you love freely. Thank you. I love you Mom.

To My Dad,

The first man I ever loved. The first man who ever loved and adored me. You still speak to my soul. I love you every day. Thank you for teaching me forgiveness. Thank you for showing me courage and reminding me of my own. I take a dose of it every day. I still fumble, but I try anyway. Thank you for blessing my life with your strength and wisdom. My heart listens for you, and peace surrounds me. I love you Dad.

TABLE OF CONTENTS

INTRODUCTION	1

PROSE

YOUR POWER	7
SURRENDER	8
EVERYTHING YOU ARE	10
GROWING BEYOND	11
LIFE	12
FOUNDATION	13
LOVE THE ONE YOU ARE	14
LOVE	15
A LIFE OF LOVE	16
TRUTH LIVES INSIDE YOU	17
LIFE IN THE WILD	18
WHO YOU ARE	19
TRUE SOURCE	20
TRAIN OF GRACE	21
NURTURING LIFE	22
LOVE IS FREEING	23
COME BACK TO LOVE	24
HEART PATH	25
SOUL TEACHERS	26
THIS IS WHERE YOU BELONG	27
BETTER FUTURE	28

POETRY

AUTHENTICITY	31
LESSONS	32
DIVINE TRUTH	33
INTUITION	34
TRUE LOVE	35
YOURS	36
YOU ARE GOLDEN	37
WHAT WE HOLD	38
YOU AREN'T BROKEN	40
INFINITY	41
FREEING YOURSELF	42
IN THE WHISPER	44
PUZZLE PEACE	45
SOUL PATH	46
A HEALED SOUL	47
HEART SIGN	48
COURAGE	49
SELF LOVE	50
STILL SHINING	51
MIRROR LOVE	52
SOUL MISSION	53
PURSUE YOUR OWN PATH	54
CHOOSING TO SEE	55
KNOWING LOVE	56
RICHNESS	57
THE STILLNESS IN YOU	58
UNIQUE	59
HELLO	60
LOVE BREATHES	61
YOUR PERSON	62
RELEASING	63
CONTAINED WITHIN	64
FLOW	65
IN SYNC	66
ALIGNMENT	67

TRANSFORMING EMOTIONS	68		FREE TO BE	104
CONNECTION	70		HEAVEN	105
ATONEMENT	71		LIFE FORCE	106
ENERGY IN MOTION	72		CELEBRATING BIRTH	107
UNSTUCK	73		THE LIGHT WITHIN	108
MOVING FROM TRUTH	74		MESSAGES	109
LITTLE YOU	76		HEALTHY LOVE	110
NEW LIFE	77		FACING YOURSELF	111
ON TAP	78		TRANSCIENCE	112
TRANSFORMATION	79		WABI SABI LOVE	113
TRANSMUTATION	80		THE I IN EVERY STORM	114
GAME OF LIFE	81		YOU ARE YOU	116
GUARDIAN OF LIGHT	82		WISDOM	117
NEW SCRIPT	83		OPEN HEART	118
YOUR WAY	84		FORGIVENESS	120
ESSENCE	85		HOME	122
DIVINE ANGELS	86		THIS LIFE	123
GUIDANCE	87		FREEDOM IN SURRENDER	124
EXPRESSION	88		WHOLENESS	126
INSPIRED CHANGE	90		DIRECTIONS	127
OPEN DOORS	92		ALL YOU	128
MEANING OF LIFE	94		RETURNING TO SOURCE	130
INNER CHILD	95		WORTHY	131
INTEGRATED	96		TRUTH BE TOLD	132
THE PATH	98		RESTORATION	134
JOY IN ALL THINGS	99		PURPOSE	135
LAUGHTER	100		GOLDEN LIGHT	136
FREE YOURSELF	101		TRUTH	137
INTEGRITY	102		ONENESS	138
CLEANING	103			

Hello! It's nice to meet you.
I'm excited to share this journey with you.

INTRODUCTION

I wrote these poems after a long period of reflection. After the loss of people in my life and through challenging experiences, I have sought to express myself in a form that I find nourishing.

I have been a Doctor in the natural health field for a long time and have witnessed people at very challenging points in their lives. I have seen people pained by inconceivable things and blessed in unthinkable ways. I know people can overcome incredible maladies. It has been an honour to support people of all ages and in various situations in unleashing freedom in their being. A life force exists within each of us that lives to create, grow, share, expand, and love.

We each have a soul path and desire to live our most fulfilling lives—the most authentic, loving embodiment of who we are. As we align with our authentic selves, may we let go, listen to our soul and move forward from that truth.

I write because my heart and soul call me to do so, and I pray my messages will give you peace and inspire your soul's path. We carry a lot of burdens, and life provides us with a lot of lessons.

These lessons come from our souls to teach and free us. Soul lessons come to us through various means. They can be experienced as physical, mental, emotional, and spiritual challenges. We are here to learn to integrate (and sometimes disintegrate) these soul lessons; in doing so, we free ourselves to move forward from a space of truth.

Soul lessons usually involve releasing energy from past experiences, false beliefs and assumptions, negative programming, societal pressures, and fears. When we become conscious and aware of our blocks, they no longer hold power over us. We are free to choose and respond with a greater understanding.

Many of these poems are about the transformative journey of breaking free from the wounds of our past and the level of consciousness that created them. These wounds can be the source of our greatest sufferings, and by releasing this wounded energy, we can live from our pureness and wholeness.

I now see challenges and unfortunate events as opportunities to discover the richness of who we are.

They guide us toward our divine consciousness; the consciousness of our sacred selves—and allow us to live life from a greater place of power and wisdom.

Lessons are openings to reframe our perceptions from a conscious perspective. A divine point of view can free and harmonize our stories from the past. Equipped with a divine understanding and awareness of truth, we can navigate through a sea of many different consciousnesses—while holding steady and true to the divine consciousness of kindness, truth, and love.

I believe that the Divine is the energy of ultimate consciousness, and through our spirit, we can connect to this divine consciousness of infinite love, truth, and wisdom. We are not separate from this divine energy, but it can move through our mind, body, spirit, and soul when we align with it—making us aware of the love and wholeness that we are.

When we get a divine nudge, inspiration, or an inner voice that gives us peace, calmness, and a grounded excitement, that is how we know we are being guided. Our soul always wants to align us with our divine consciousness, the *integrated* us.

As we move from this truth, we move from our inner heart wisdom that knows.

Please enjoy this collection of prose and poems written to inspire, uplift, and encourage us all to follow our soul path, a unique journey of self-discovery and spiritual growth. The undercurrent of each poem reflects the soul's endeavours to free us through our connection to our divine inner wisdom.

Love does heal all woes. To love is a choice naturally accessed when we surrender to our divine consciousness. As we follow our inner heart wisdom, remain humble, find forgiveness, choose gratitude, and return to love, our every moment will access this divine flow.

Your future awaits. Free your soul.

PROSE

YOUR POWER

May you choose people who care for your soul. Let them show up for you and nurture your heart. Forgive them when they offer an apology from their heart. Forgive them when they lack awareness and knowledge of their ignorance. Learn to value and respect those who support you and love the person you are. Be grateful for the ones who journey with you through thick and thin. Appreciate the souls who will hug and hold you until you catch your breath again. Be held. Receive love. Be grateful, and choose to be there for them when the time comes.

SURRENDER

We gain power over our disease when we harness the roots of our pain. Pain weeps for someone to listen. It needs to be heard and acknowledged. Pain carries a message that, when grasped, will offer more understanding about who we are and what we need. Throughout life, the brave journey of growth, parts of us will need mending. Self-understanding brings us freedom, layer by layer. We learn things will fall onto our path, and sometimes they will trip us, but every challenge can aid our power if we allow it. By meeting and acknowledging our pain, we surrender to our wholeness. The path to self-discovery is sometimes mired in pain and landmines. Let us be gentle and permit ourselves to look at all that causes us pain—perhaps a sideways glance to begin but with the intention of releasing what pains us. Each attempt will draw us closer to the truth as we face ourselves more directly.

Each time we use life to free ourselves, we allow it to build our inner strength.

muriel okubo

One day the things that bother us will no longer. The things that challenge us will have become the beautifully woven tapestry of our soul.

EVERYTHING YOU ARE

Let integrity and kindness reveal your soul, and give because you have been blessed. Care because you know despair. Love because you know fear. Among those you will encounter, some will be delivered as gifts, and many more wrapped as lessons. With every moment, remember who you are. Wherever you go, leave behind the memory of your essence. Bless each moment with love, as that embodies all you are and all our world needs.

GROWING BEYOND

We make soul agreements before we arrive on Earth. For most of us, our first teachers are our parents. We are born to this earth—a burst of creation infused with love. Someone gave birth to us, and now, that life is ours. Let us follow an enlightened path, be joyful for blessings, and be mindful of patterns with the power to alter our way. We can create new awareness and understanding as we walk our soul path with reverence. Let us use everything as kindling for growth, stay conscious of what is ours, and be generous with the rest. Design and create a life with all our heart. Find wisdom in a blade of grass and our grandfathers' eyes. The power lies in our choices. Take only what serves us and bless the things not for us. In our journey, all things can be enriched with love.

You, my dear, are loved.

free your soul

LIFE

Discover who you are, the person you were meant to be. Embody a life defined by your divine alignment. Overflow with vibrance. Heaven is within. Be discerning what seeks to penetrate you, and mindfully label what to return to the sender. Set down your burdens and let go of the pressures that bruise your spirit. Navigate each day with more ease, truth, and grace. Energy constantly moves, and the world around you makes demands of you in many ways. Understand this is part of the dance. Shine, discern, and release as you uncover the truth. Do this over and over again. This is the practice of life, the practice of love. Be you through all of it.

FOUNDATION

What we perceive as failures are often significant bridges to our success—allowing us to tap into our true heart's wisdom and move from that clarity. Sometimes, it takes the perfect storm to break us down in the right ways, showing us what isn't solid and sustainable—and guiding us back to our natural alignment. Our souls yearn for peace, signalling distress when our spirit is depressed. So, the next time we encounter failure, let it be a powerful reminder that our souls want us to reconnect to our passion for expressing our heart's authenticity.

LOVE THE ONE YOU ARE

Throughout life, people will leave— some by choice, some by design, some by will. Choose always to love yourself, no matter who or what you encounter. All of us move toward the final gate. You, too, will leave at the perfect moment; in the meantime, life is more enjoyable when you love. Carry love and leave all fear behind. When people leave, let them go. Love comes to us and sometimes moves on. Enjoy it through every moment. You have more than enough love, so love more and love again. When people stay, delight in their presence and amplify the love. Embrace what is. This is the glory of love and life. One of the few things guaranteed in life is that love exists right now for you. Be present with love. Be love.

LOVE

Learn to love. Grow comfortable with it. Learn to love your troubles and love the lessons they reveal. In this way, you will know how to love and be loved. Witness what love is and what it is not. Come to the edge of love. Fall in love. Dance in love. Cry in love. Love is the only thing you have come here to learn. If you learn anything, let it be love. You will have succeeded once you have been wrung out, and love is all there is.

A LIFE OF LOVE

Wisdom tells us love is all there is. In the fabric of life, we are all woven in love. Because we love, we are made stronger and more beautiful. Let us mend all our layers with love to love more deeply and give more freely. Life exists because of love and would cease to exist without it.

TRUTH LIVES INSIDE YOU

The truth you hold within gives you a foundation of wisdom, safety, strength, beauty, clarity, and love. If you are uncertain in your external world, understand that your internal world can be accessed anytime. Don't look to the world for the truth because everything starts with you. True wisdom comes from a centred heart that has eyes to see and ears to hear. When you know this truth, your energy will hold your truth, and it will harmonize both worlds.

LIFE IN THE WILD

To make meaning of your life, take space and see it from a distance and in stillness. Find peace within yourself. Surrender to the unknown. Embrace the unfolding. When you live this way, the meaning of life, especially *your* life, will naturally come to you. More joy and more love will give birth to miracles. Be kind with your heart as it opens and explores. What is right will be freeing for your soul. Give love freely, bringing people with positive energy into your life. Creativity will give birth to further clarity. Let it launch your strong will and inspire your growth. You are on the right path. Follow your heart, and it will lead you to your wildest dreams. Live and love in the wild.

WHO YOU ARE

Loveable, loved, abundant, beautiful, unique, worthy, exceptional, powerful, capable, wise, safe, valuable, unlimited. These qualities are inherent in your essence. They were birthed and infused into you. They are inseparable from who you are. They need not be created, nor can they be destroyed. They can never be taken away. In need of nothing, you come fully prepared and fully equipped. Remember these truths when you need to be reminded of who you are. Truth can't be erased. The truth is imprinted in your soul. Surrender to who you are.

TRUE SOURCE

We all have to discover our true source of love. In this way, we can truly love from a place of abundance and cultivate it within ourselves on demand. When we give and receive from a heart of fullness, everything can expand and grow with health and vitality.

TRAIN OF GRACE

You are not here to suffer nor to hold on to discord. Some things are not yours, and you have the power to let them fall away. You will miss your train of grace if you get distracted by the trains, *not* on your schedule. Grace is here to usher you to your desired destiny. Set your eyes toward heaven, and remember what is yours. What do you want? What is yours will be yours. No forcing. No pushing. Grace will flow, stop before you and open its doors to you. Let the trains that are not yours make their way past you, allowing the energy to move through you with peace, love, and freedom. Board the train that aligns with the essence of you. Let grace befall you and take you on the ride of your life.

NURTURING LIFE

Life requires nurturing. All fruit starts as a seed. Given the right conditions, time, and care, it will start to sprout. Imagine the beauty it possesses. Watch what it needs. One day, at the perfect time, it will sprout and blossom. And then keep nurturing it through life.

LOVE IS FREEING

The moment we feel worthy of love is the moment we no longer need to control anything. We can experience the colours of emotions while seeing the humour of it all. We are fascinating, beautiful people. We can respect someone's choices because we all thrive in freedom. The freedom to find ourselves, to walk the path of our choice. The freedom to be. Unencumbered by pressure, we discover the truth within. Even in moments of sadness, we can be happy for the balance of life. We wouldn't want it any other way. Aligned souls will choose each other. The soul has a way of knowing long before we do. Let our soul reveal those that resonate with us. When our soul meets a kindred spirit, we will feel more freedom than ever before. I choose this for all of us. I choose this for eternity.

COME BACK TO LOVE

When faced with a disease, we seek answers outside of ourselves. Everything that fails as an antidote is an indication to seek for the cure within. The disease is a disturbance to our wholeness. We begin to heal when we discover that love is the answer to our wholeness. With kindness, forgiveness, and deliberate release from the things that wound us, our problems begin to lose their power. Take time to listen to the whisper of intuition. What do we need? Why did we need this disease? Worry not about what other people think. Surrender to love and watch fear vanish. As we learn to love ourselves back to wholeness again, including the parts we feel are undeserving, disease will move further away. Love will fill in all the spaces we will allow. Let's not stop until every last bit is accounted for and make ample space to show where we need to love and where we need to release.

HEART PATH

As you follow your true heart path, you will experience peace and contentment. Your mind, body, and soul will move as one, and you will begin to feel your limitlessness. Your energy will flow...

So go and leave your golden trail of love. Let your purpose animate everything you do. Say yes to letting your heart choose.

SOUL TEACHERS

There will be people who come across your path with sage advice. They speak your soul's language, sharing the truth—things you already know. You will remember the essence of what they told you because they are calling on the courage they know you have. You may or may not follow the wisdom, depending on your ability to embrace it. Soul teachers give evergreen messages— and when you are ready, you can revisit their words to process, discern, and contemplate them deeply because their message is still what you need. It's not too late to follow your heart and the truth of your soul. Soul teachers are part of your tribe— they see your soul's light, the wholeness you embody, and love you to your depths. You are more mature and wise now to know the truth, and to listen to the wisdom of your heart. Let the message move you forward in your life. You weren't ready then, but you are now. Let the power of love in the wisdom of words change your life. You are ready now.

THIS IS WHERE YOU BELONG

Learn to let go of people who make your heart feel oppressed. They will deplete the richness of your moments and dim your light. Your emotional and spiritual battery will drain until you feel more dead than alive. Trust in the intuition that tells you of your intrinsic worth. Rejoice in being true to yourself. Learn to care enough for yourself to know when to leave and when to stay. Listen to the beat of your heart and remain open to love. Stand in your golden hue wherever you go—welcome fellow travellers who embrace and respect your light. Your heart's truth will clear the path forward. Let the energy flow. This is your natural state. This is where you belong.

BETTER FUTURE

We are all moving from our present state of consciousness. Our past holds our past consciousness. We can step into a better future as we embrace a greater consciousness.

POETRY

AUTHENTICITY

Release everything that isn't you—
your generational traumas,
your inner child wounds,
your limiting beliefs,
your fears,
your insecurities,
your core negative cognitions.
They are not you,
they never were.
Now you are free
to live untethered,
as the most wholesome you.
You are divine,
you are free
because you choose to be free.

LESSONS

You are meant to be here.
To learn the lessons.
To be hurt.
To learn to soothe your suffering.
You are meant to be challenged
by certain things—
sometimes, it isn't all that graceful,
but looking back,
you have learned a lot.
The future is lived forward
and without the past lessons,
you wouldn't have the chance
to choose the future
that you want.
Love forward,
my friend.

DIVINE TRUTH

The truth sets us free.
In truth—
we are love,
we are loved,
we are whole,
we are beautiful,
we are worthy,
we are creators.
If this is the truth,
what are the possibilities for our lives?

INTUITION

We can only see patterns
after we have lived through
many experiences.
This is the blessing of life—
it shows us the knowledge
and wisdom we have gained,
and the power we have
in creating our lives.
Sometimes, we will find
ourselves in new situations
in which we have no understanding
of what to do or where to go.
In these times,
may we lean into our intuition
and be guided by
our divine consciousness
that is rooting for us
to live our lives in the best
possible way.
Surrender to the possibilities,
and a gentle comfort will arise.
Make space for the truth,
and grace will fill it.
This is our power and gift.

muriel okubo

TRUE LOVE

Be true to the most loving part of yourself,
as you live as an authentic being.
God is working miracles in your life.
Have the wisdom to know;
sometimes, people will not stay,
sometimes, people are removed
from your path,
sometimes, you have the courage
and the discernment needed to walk away.
When something feels uneasy in your soul,
stop!
Divinely protected and aware,
you can discover those who—
love you,
cherish you,
respect you,
and those who will honour your love.
Love resonates with love.
True love will be a mirror for you
and will remind you that love is
everlasting,
infinite,
and free.

free your soul

YOURS

Beautiful things cannot be forced
or controlled—
that person's heart,
that person's choice,
that person's love.
When beautiful things are forced
or controlled,
they aren't beautiful anymore.
The beauty meant for you
will match the beauty you bring,
and that culmination will naturally bring
a greater beauty—
one of fullness,
one of rejoicing,
one of deep love and expansion.
Beautiful things will flow
and will resonate with you.
There is beauty that is yours
awaiting you on the other side of letting go
of what is not yours.

muriel okubo

YOU ARE GOLDEN

Sweet soul,
what are you still holding on to?
Release your burdens.
Honour your soul.
Give yourself permission
to forgive yourself.
You came to be a light
in an enormity and magnitude.
Love will flow to the degree you allow.
Grow in love,
shine as bright as you can
and, as you do,
your radiance will call forth
an abundance of love
always and forever.

WHAT WE HOLD

When we were children,
we faced many things thrust into our world.
Some things left us wounded,
and other things enhanced our power.
The framework of life
gets set into our belief system.
As adults, we take these beliefs
and navigate the world.
Sometimes, we encounter events
that hyper-irritate these wounds;
and sometimes, it feels effortless.
Based on our lens,
we make assessments, assumptions,
and automatic interpretations
to keep us safe from perceived harm.
We are largely unconscious
of the things we do
and why we do them
because it is encoded into our being.
When the time is right,
we can gently observe and contemplate
the beliefs we hold—
beliefs about ourselves,
the possibilities for our lives,

muriel okubo

and what is divinely true.
Perhaps we would evaluate
how the pain was installed
and the meaning
we gave to those experiences.
Our future depends on it.
The future depends on us
to look beneath the surface
to see what is true.
This is something we can do
to use the love that is our birthright
and free ourselves.
Little by little,
love will transform our beliefs
into those aligned with divinity,
the whole truth of who we are,
the destiny that always belonged to us.

YOU AREN'T BROKEN

Sometimes, we need to be reminded
that we aren't broken.
It is the world that puts these ideas
in our heads.
We are merely whole people,
that have had experiences that pained us
in the past.
Pain comes with the territory
here on Earth.
This doesn't mean
there is anything wrong with us
because we feel intensely and deeply.
Pain doesn't break us,
it only shows us
there is a spirit inside,
having to respond to it all.
We are not broken;
it is the world we live in.
We are not the painful experience,
merely the experiencer that must
make art with all that comes our way.

INFINITY

All possibilities exist
in a frequency of love.

FREEING YOURSELF

As you release the trapped, wounded energy
you held in your body and consciousness
for so long,
like an old friend,
they were comfortable,
but not lifting you higher.
You had become used to thinking
they were helping you.
In your deception, you couldn't fathom
that they held you down.
It became a story
that anchored you to lies.
Lies that said you couldn't move on,
lies that said you weren't enough,
lies that said you don't deserve love,
lies that said you're not important,
lies that said you're unworthy
of your desires,
and, as you stopped embracing them,
you ceased entertaining their slights,
you started recognizing your wounds,
allowing the rawness to disintegrate.
You don't believe you need them anymore.
You served them many times,

but you are no longer their servant.
You take all your power back,
unapologetically and assuredly.
You let them go with love and compassion.
You release them to release you.
You are free.

IN THE WHISPER

When challenged by choice,
close your door and sit peacefully.
Choose the path that ignites
and inspires your soul.
How does it feel,
and do you want to experience more?
More is an indication of energy
that needs to move there,
and if you never want to go there again,
it is the other,
choose the one that lets your heartbeat
in rhythms of truth, peace, and joy—
creating a grounded excitement.
Let your being expand on the wings
of a golden, inspired breath lined with love
that only your heart will know.

PUZZLE PEACE

We are all great creators,
but there is providence
when we create from a heart-led place.
Our hearts know the truth of our souls
and it's with this wisdom
we can live from
a place of gratitude,
meaning,
and wholeness.
Each of us,
were divinely created;
possessing unique gifts
that are beyond our understanding.
It's our purpose to find
our place in the world
that gives us the most peace
in our being.

SOUL PATH

Sometimes, we have to choose
a new soul path,
and sometimes, the world won't like it.
Often, there are patterns we need
to grow beyond—
to go another way.
Oh course,
we will grieve
and hurt in the absence of the familiar.
Fear will sometimes call us back
to the old ways.
Taking a turn
can often mean that we have discovered,
we would rather lose parts of our life
than lose our souls.
Destiny will call us,
and the path will beckon us forward
to become more
than our pasts can allow.

muriel okubo

A HEALED SOUL

A soul that is cared for, heals.
A soul that is cared for, remembers
who they are.
A soul that is cared for, embraces
their wholeness.

HEART SIGN

When you are anxious,
identify the place in your body
that you feel it.
Don't try to make it go away—
put your loving presence on it;
let it expand,
let it move,
let it breathe,
let it tell you its story.
By giving you this signal,
it is asking for your presence
and your love.
Nothing more.
Stay calm and watch it—
don't feed it.
It only wants you
to hold space for it.
In doing so,
you will get a message of truth—
inner heart wisdom
that will free you with
a message of peace.

muriel okubo

COURAGE

Courage is not the absence of fear
but moving forward in its presence.
It takes courage
to face what lies ahead,
to receive the desires of your heart,
to feel worthy of success,
to move on after rejection,
to forgive yourself,
to forgive others,
to trust yourself after heartbreak,
to try again after failure,
to ask out your crush,
to be vulnerable with your truth,
to find the energy to create a new path,
to pick yourself up again,
to truly live with passion,
to discover your purpose,
to love with no conditions,
to look at your fears and see the truth.
Forge ahead, courageous one,
and let your destiny unfold.

SELF LOVE

The good stuff of life
all begins when we lovingly
accept ourselves.
We can live a peaceful life
in unity and integrity
to the truth of who we are.
We can live and die
while honouring our souls.
This is a life well lived;
this is a light that death cannot extinguish;
this is the journey of self-love.

STILL SHINING

In an age of information and censorship,
it becomes essential
to discover the truth within.
It's okay to be different,
it's okay for people not to understand you,
it's okay to discover opposition,
it's okay that you disagree with your peers.
This paradigm is the nature
of a world operating
from different levels of consciousness.
We would all know absolute truths
in the ideal world,
allowing for exponential growth
and expansion.
You have to be the one
who is okay with your decisions;
you have to be okay with the consequences;
you have to be okay with who you are.
You have to find
what nourishes your light.
Flame the fire within.
The truth will carry you through
and in the end,
are you true to your heart?

MIRROR LOVE

Find someone who looks at you
to see you.
Find someone who listens to you
to hear you.
Find someone who embraces you
to receive you.
Find someone who touches you
to feel you.
Find someone who waits for you
to know you.
Find someone who cares for you
to comfort you.
And when you find that someone,
who holds you with respect and love,
know you are
one with this love—
this gift of love that mirrors your soul.

muriel okubo

SOUL MISSION

Please stand in your truth;
you have nothing to fear.
Show up as you are,
and the world will greet you.
Sometimes it will like you,
and sometimes it won't.
There is strength in authenticity.
The world is not your measuring stick.
Stand in the love of your divinity—
this is your soul mission.
This is your sole mission.

PURSUE YOUR OWN PATH

Don't believe everything you hear;
seek for your soul's clarity.
It doesn't matter if the world
tells you differently;
what matters is what your soul tells you.
Trust your inner knowing,
and seek to know your authentic self.
The kingdom of heaven is within;
the answers are always there
to lead and guide you along the divine path.
As you honour the truth
and wisdom of your heart,
your choices will free your soul.

CHOOSING TO SEE

When we take our blinders off
and choose to see ourselves
through the eyes of clarity and truth,
we will discover—
our worthiness,
our value,
our wholeness,
and our peace.
This is the pathway to our freedom—
freedom from distortion,
freedom from the world.
Through our divine vision,
we will know unconditional love,
and the truth of our soul.

KNOWING LOVE

I wish for you to get used
to good people in your life—
to get used to trusting someone,
to needing someone,
to not have to be perfect,
to have someone have your back.
I want these for you
all the time,
every time,
all at once,
forever.
I want you to be surrounded by healers
on your journey to remind you
of your wholeness
and that love is limitless.
These are the people who are;
food for your soul,
the template for life's blessings,
the kindling for more greatness,
and love nesting love.

RICHNESS

Your authentic self
chooses love, peace, and kindness—
the truth and currency of your soul.

THE STILLNESS IN YOU

I wish for you to be able to sit in silence
and for you to enjoy your own company.
I hope you are not afraid to like
and love yourself—
to know that silence
can free you of anxiety and panic
when you befriend yourself.
May it give you the space
to witness your beauty,
your strength,
your innocence,
your vulnerability,
your wholeness.
In the stillness,
may your heart find peace
in yourself.

muriel okubo

UNIQUE

What you have,
no one else has.
No one can do what you do,
like you do.
Be seen,
be heard,
be known.
When you are focused
on what you have to give,
you can give with an unfiltered heart.
You can be your soul on purpose.

HELLO

Surrender to this knowingness—
the best is unfolding in front of you.
Embrace everything
with your presence.
There is a divine plan for your life,
and you are equipped
with everything you need.
Find what flames your fire,
and rise with that energy that
flows from within.
Your energy will show you
where to move because your
life force wants to grow and appreciate.
Immerse yourself in the places
that make you feel alive,
and high-spirited.
This is your life in flow.

LOVE BREATHES

The right people will feel safe for you
at all levels of your being—
spiritually, mentally, emotionally,
and physically.
You don't have to negotiate
with any of these
to make them fit.
The right people will naturally
align with you
and you with them.
There is a beautiful love wiggle
between you.
Your relationship will be a home
that breathes,
allows for growth and expansion,
and creates space to love and be free.

YOUR PERSON

Find someone whom you deeply respect
and admire.
Someone who smiles at you,
and the whole world disappears.
Someone who is your best friend
and shares belly laughs.
Someone you can be conscious with
and someone you can be unconscious with.
Find arms that feel like home,
someone who is passionate
and excited about you and by you.
Someone who can swim deep with you
and loves and adores the heart of your soul.
Someone who wants to grow with you
and defaults to kindness,
especially when inconvenient.
This is the love of your worth.

RELEASING

Let go of the story
to free yourself.

CONTAINED WITHIN

And in gratitude, there is forgiveness,
and in forgiveness, there is peace,
and in peace, there is love,
and in love, there is freedom,
and in freedom, there is truth,
and in truth, there is alignment,
and in alignment, there is God,
and in God, there is you.

muriel okubo

FLOW

The natural flow of all things
must be respected.
What is best for us
will not have to be forced.
Allow your inherent nature to rise
and meet the truth of your soul.

IN SYNC

Being in alignment with our soul
is a beautiful thing.
There is space for movement
yet a foundation of stability,
a sense of "rightness" in our being,
an integrity in the flow,
a currency of love and truth,
and the peace of atonement.

muriel okubo

ALIGNMENT

When we are in alignment,
there is a grace
in making the right decisions,
in choosing the right people,
in going to the right places,
in seeing with discernment,
and speaking our authentic truth.
We can show up as our true selves
and experience harmonic resonance.

TRANSFORMING EMOTIONS

It is the body's wisdom
to feel certain events
and situations,
and often, our emotions can overwhelm
our free-spirited nature.
Different emotions can get stuck
in our energy field;
leading our bodies to retain these energies.
Our souls feel most at peace,
when we are experiencing love,
enjoying ourselves,
and when things are calm.
We can return to our divine, loving nature
by allowing the energy
to be felt,
and supported in their movement.
In doing this practice of transformation,
we can free the burdens on our hearts
by restoring ourselves
with freedom and ease.
Feel the emotions—
honour them,
respect them,
and give them space to breathe.

muriel okubo

In their expression,
our capacity to love
becomes limitless and open once again.
It is here the soul rejoices.

CONNECTION

Take space to become aligned.
Sit tall,
breathe,
connect to the light within,
feel the love within,
be the love within,
be your authentic self,
listen deeply to your soul.

ATONEMENT

The things that are right for you
will be in alignment with your soul—
the part of you that is deeply loved
and loving.
There will be no confusion
or dishonouring of your soul.
It doesn't mean there aren't storms,
but there is a knowingness
that the true path gives your heart peace.
True love will line your path
as you follow your heart.
This divine step will lead to the next.
Walk the path of greater joy, love, peace,
and freedom.

ENERGY IN MOTION

When an emotion arises,
and the sensation makes you feel
like you are being chased, overwhelmed,
or swallowed,
take time to understand
what you are
perceiving or interpreting.
Emotions are a gift to free yourself
and your soul.
Let the emotion ride out,
and return you to love—
in this process,
of staying present,
you will be able to let go
and surrender to your wholeness.
Energy moves in waves
and between each emotion;
your conscious awareness
is your anchor to peace.

muriel okubo

UNSTUCK

When we are ready,
we can boldly open wounds—
giving ourselves freedom
from misguided thoughts and beliefs,
unhealthy agreements, discord,
confusion, hurt, and regret.
Most of these wounds,
were created in a time and place
when our energy was compromised,
and we lacked the support to be authentic.
In a space of compassion,
we can peel back these wounds
and slowly disintegrate
the hold they have on us.
Restoration can be found by;
feeling the wounds in our bodies,
listening to their truths,
and lovingly caring for each one.
Immerse each wound
with a divine consciousness
of love, truth and presence.
In attending to our unmet needs,
we can free ourselves of the
burdens we carry.

free your soul

MOVING FROM TRUTH

Everything we do in our lives,
will have consequences—
which can be reassuring,
encouraging,
liberating,
depressing,
disheartening,
fill-in-the-blank.
When you are deciding between
different choices or actions—
whatever it is,
choose from a place of inner
high-spiritedness—
an energy that embodies
love, truth, peace and clarity.
It is okay to ask for higher guidance.
If we create some space to listen,
we will get a nudge,
a voice,
an inspiration.
Move with it.
Move from it.
The next step will reveal itself.
Hotter...

muriel okubo

Colder...
Step away...
Reevaluate...
Study more...
Go forward...
There is no rush to make these choices,
even when it seems like there is pressure.
The things that require
immediate attention,
we will do without thought—
the things that don't require
immediate attention
are everything else.
The things that are out of our control
will not ask us to do anything.
The things that are in our control,
will be the things that are asking us
to dig for our soul's truth.
Aligning with the peace in our hearts,
will reveal the way.

free your soul

LITTLE YOU

Be committed to make
your inner child
proud of you—
to have them know you care for them,
to have them know
you will protect them,
to have them know
you will work toward your dreams
with your whole heart,
to have them know they are seen.
Be committed to show them
that you love them
and will never stop.

muriel okubo

NEW LIFE

When you release trauma from the past,
and realize it doesn't need
to be processed anymore,
you can lay down your energetic sword.
This is a day that you will discover
a new life—
a life that is yours,
a life propelled and powered
by divine inspiration,
a life that can be birthed anew.
What will you do with this new power,
where will you go,
what will you experience?
This is a day to rejoice
and let love lead the way.

free your soul

ON TAP

Our divine nature
holds truth, strength, wisdom, and love.
We have everything we need
to face the darkest moments
of our lives.
When we are facing
a painful season of life,
please remember we hold the light
to shine our way through.
This divine life force is within us
and surrounding us.
We can tap into it whenever
and wherever we
are in need.

TRANSFORMATION

We are here,
we are present,
we yearn to know more.
We are on this journey to live the truth.
As we uncover more,
our lives change for the better.
The truth will always bring better.
The truth does set us free
from the darkness.
To get to the truth,
we often have to face our fears.
Fear feels like a monster
because we misunderstand it.
In being open to our fears,
we see the places
where we lack understanding,
and through our witness
we can walk a new path of freedom.
When we shine a light on our fears—
light transmutes the dark,
restoring love.
Love is the base to which all things return.
We are here to choose.

free your soul

TRANSMUTATION

When you bring forth your light,
you shine so brightly;
you illuminate life.
Refrain from diming yourself,
because you never know
who needs your light.
Light heals,
light saves,
light shows us where to go,
light gives us life,
light will reveal the truth,
light brings freedom.
In the presence of light,
we see more than before.
In the presence of light,
we love more than before.
In the presence of light,
love transmutes fear.
Be the light.

GAME OF LIFE

Don't be afraid to do things
you are called to do—
the things pulling on your heartstrings
that give you joy.
This life is yours to create.
Remember, there is only one of you,
and the world needs your unique light.
You have a precious life
and you are meant to live it in a way
that brings out more of your light.
So, take the risk,
if you fail,
you will learn to try again.
That's what this life is...
creating, growing, and expanding.
When you hit a roadblock,
that's okay, breathe,
and let your energy build again.
Don't give up on the desires of your heart;
know that this world is an obstacle course
that doesn't have anything against you
personally,
so keep going after what you want,
and remember, it's part of the game of life.

free your soul

GUARDIAN OF LIGHT

You can only hold on to
your principles.
You can't control what another person
thinks or does.
You can only hold true to the beauty
and love that inhabits your soul.
You must be the guardian
of the light you hold.
Don't let the world
change this part of you.
Protect the truth,
protect your heart,
protect your soul,
protect your love.
Stay true to the love in your heart.

NEW SCRIPT

I wish for you to always remember
that every time you feel upset,
uneasy or anxious;
there is a story that you need to release.
These stories are not the truth
of who you are.
So go ahead,
release what was never yours,
and accept the responsibility of what is—
your ability to respond.
Move from the truth
and let the divine work through you
to bring out the best of who you are.

YOUR WAY

Don't get discouraged by the past—
whatever you believe
should have been done differently,
the past is your wisdom.
You did the best you could
with the information you had.
Moving forward,
please take what you have learned
to live more fully.
Given what you know now,
what do you think you will do?
Cherish good relationships.
Stay calm through duress.
Choose love over fear.
Find peace before acting.
Ask for help from wise counsel.
Discern from different perspectives.
Stay open to possibility.
Take a chance at something
that brings you excitement.
Release the story of the past and be present
to the inner wisdom of your heart.
There is a beautiful story waiting
for you to write it.

muriel okubo

ESSENCE

Precious child,
your skin so soft,
your eyes so bright,
your laugh so pure,
you are a miracle.
If you can take anything with you,
please keep your light
and the love in your heart
and the kindness of your soul.

DIVINE ANGELS

When we decide to change our lives,
divine nudges will catch our attention
to move us forward.
We will meet angels on our paths,
we will go to places that heal our souls,
we will have conversations
that expand our realities,
we will meet people who open our hearts,
we will feel shifts that click within our souls.
Our angels are here to help when we ask,
divinely guiding us to walk through
the right doors.
Be excited,
be grateful.
The divine path is
opening just for us.

GUIDANCE

Signs and synchronicities,
miracles and messages,
peace and freedom—
this is available,
this is your path,
this is divine resonance.

EXPRESSION

Pain,
shame,
guilt,
sadness,
anxiety,
anger,
fear,
and insecurity
can manifest as
uncomfortable emotions
in our bodies.
Uncomfortable emotions
carry many stories from the past—
often negative beliefs
that are seeking
expression and release.
With presence and love,
we can give ourselves,
the guidance to free ourselves
from the events and energies
that got lodged into our bodies
when we had a limited perspective.

muriel okubo

With maturity, skill, support,
patience, and nurturance,
we can release these charged energies.

INSPIRED CHANGE

When we are wounded,
we will see from distortion.
Light isn't as bright,
colours aren't as vibrant,
clouds loom overhead.
We can't hold a full charge,
and darkness holds more comfort.
Then we ask for change.
We see a flash of light,
called to do different things—
talk to a stranger,
book a flight,
go on a new adventure.
Everything changes.
That spark will heal our wounds;
inspiration will mend our hearts
and remind us that we were never lacking.
We are beautiful beings
with everything we always needed.
We can now see
from a space of enlightenment.
Today is the birth of the new us.
We are free.
This is our gift.

muriel okubo

Be now,
go now,
love now.
The cosmos is a place
for constant renewal
and divine inspiration.

OPEN DOORS

Don't struggle to open doors
that aren't meant for you.
The key you have fits the locks
that are for you—
don't ignore the nudge
or the whisper to let go.
Stop pushing,
navigate away from the murky waters,
pause,
listen,
trust,
and have courage.
Your soul is leading you in the right way
to calm shores,
the beautiful, fulfilling path.
Your soul knows
the who,
the what,
the when,
the where,
the why,
and the how.
Your soul knows you,

muriel okubo

your key is special and unique.
The right doors will open you
to greater joy, love, peace and freedom.

MEANING OF LIFE

Our physical bodies will one day
decompose.
Our spiritual body,
will continue to live.
The things of this world are temporary—
our struggles,
the money we earn,
our egos,
the material things,
the control systems of this world.
If we can live from the perspective
of our eternal soul,
it will be easier to manage
the temporary limitations of this world.
We are the only ones
who can make meaning of our lives—
let's live it true to the essence
and soul of who we are.

muriel okubo

INNER CHILD

When tragedy hits at a young age,
we experience situations
where we endure unmet needs.
Not until we are ready
will we hear our inner child calling,
asking to connect
to care for it in the ways it needs.
And when we are ready,
we can unite with comfort, care, and love.
Our inner child will talk with us—
we become mother and father.
Our inner child is not separate
but wants to be integrated
into who we are now.
Love, affection, support, and attention
will connect and free us both.
Nothing is left to do.
We can dance and play
in the rich, total abundance
of our destiny together—
gleefully, freely, and in wholeness.
Integrated,
we can step forward
in peace and holiness.

free your soul

INTEGRATED

The parts we find triggering and difficult
are the parts of us
waiting to be integrated with love.
At some point,
we believed there was unfairness,
and it created dissonance within us.
Events, people, and situations will arise
to teach us to love these parts
back to wholeness.
We can't change what happened.
The world we experience
has been laid with a pattern.
By changing the energy and perspective
of the inequity,
we may choose to see the world
with a new integrity.
We may change the frequency of our grid
by applying a new vision of choice,
a life we fancy.
The trajectory of our destiny
can now be made
into one of more love,

more kindness,
more compassion,
and more truth.

THE PATH

Please remember
your light is your lamp—
your path forward.
How will you know where to go?
You must always hold your light.
Light will grow exponentially.
A tiny bit of light
is all that is needed to dispel darkness.
One itty bitty light can be kindling
for another person's light.
Light attracts light.
Light will build.
Walk in the light.
In light, our path will be lit.
In the light of truth,
all will be revealed.

muriel okubo

JOY IN ALL THINGS

Joyfully let the people
who don't love you, leave.
Joyfully let the people
who reject you, depart.
Joyfully let the people
who don't want you, flee.
Joyfully let the people
who choose someone over you,
move on.
Joyfully accept all these things
because you have to make space
for all the people who want to
love you,
hold you,
keep you,
embrace you,
and never let you go.

LAUGHTER

The sound of laughter
is a beautiful thing.
It is the sound of the heart
vibrating in tandem with joy.
Your heart was made to laugh.
Hear it often.
It will save you a million times over.
Do you think laughter
can cure diseases of the heart?

FREE YOURSELF

Until you confront your fears,
you remain their prisoner.
It can be subtle,
lying dormant in the background.
Love can free you.
Will you let it?
When you do the thing you fear,
because it is guided from your loving heart,
fear vanishes,
and grace grows.
The fear cycle ends,
and the movement of love flows.

INTEGRITY

The inner aligner—
what you say,
what you do,
where you go.
Inner wholeness,
outer truth—
this is the agreement of your soul.

CLEANING

There will always be things that come up
to clean our vibration—
it can be a traumatic event,
an illness,
a difficult relationship,
a global pandemic.
Whatever we face
allows us to look within
and determine what part of us
wants to identify with the stories
that keep us in bondage,
and those that will free us.
Consider this a reset.

FREE TO BE

Life is full of tough choices.
Everyone has a different history
that is propelling their present,
and everyone is doing what is meaningful
from their perspective.
Our consciousness is like a river
returning to the sea.
Our ultimate power lies
in becoming in tune
with the ocean of
divine consciousness—
the place of our freedom.
As we make our way,
let our every step
come from this truth.

muriel okubo

HEAVEN

Earth school is an exciting place—
everyone has a purpose to be here;
your heart mission.
If you could bring heaven on earth here,
what would you do?

LIFE FORCE

When your heart wisdom
is moving your energy in a particular
direction,
you can put your entire being
into all that you do.
All great works
require much discipline.
Don't be discouraged
when it get's tough;
let everything come at you
and move forward steadily
to create your path.
Take a step forward every day,
and behind you
will be every mountain
you overcame.

muriel okubo

CELEBRATING BIRTH

You didn't come here to live a mediocre life.
You came here to be everything
you want to be.
There will always be forces
that will go against you,
and that is precisely
what you must remember
when facing challenges.
Most things you believe
are not necessarily true.
You can craft a life
based on the truth.
When you add your stitching of love,
truth, honesty, and integrity—
you add to the fabric of this world.
This world needs you
in your fullness,
in your wholeness,
and in your uniqueness.
Don't play small anymore.
You have got what no one else
on this planet has.
Remember the things that light you up
and don't let anything put you out.

THE LIGHT WITHIN

Spending your time outward-focussed,
you wondered why you felt
so lonely and dark.
By trying to fulfill yourself
with the external world,
you would remain separate from yourself.
As you quieted your mind,
you learned you didn't need to
chase a cure,
chase money,
chase relationships,
chase control.
Behind all the chasing—
you had a desire for love, security,
health, wealth and freedom—
which are inherent in the richness
of who you are.
You didn't need to chase
what you already had.
In humility, you met
the divine healer within
and allowed yourself to be discovered.
You are the lighthouse,
You are love.

muriel okubo

MESSAGES

Soul messages sound
a lot like this:
open your heart,
move forward with courage,
surrender to the moment,
follow your heart wisdom,
be thankful for this journey,
seek the truth,
love.
What do you hear?

HEALTHY LOVE

When love comes into your life,
connect with your heart
and be infused with breath and life.
Healthy love will feel like steady sunshine
after spring rain.
Feel the brightness.
It will be everything
your past trauma was not,
carrying with it lightness and truth.
Don't block yourself,
sabotaging what may come.
Open your heart fully
to see with God's clarity
and welcome everything your soul desires.
If it is true,
healthy love,
it will hold an undercurrent
of unfaltering kindness.
When two healed hearts come together,
they are both set free.

muriel okubo

FACING YOURSELF

When you face yourself,
you have nowhere to hide.
You can try,
but most often,
you will fail.
The parts that need your attention
will make you aware
until you go blind.
When you get tired of hurting yourself,
running and tripping over the same blocks,
this is where you decide
whether you continue to stay blind
or choose to open your eyes.
In this pivotal moment,
you uncover the beauty you always had
but were too scared to witness.
Waste not a minute longer.
Face yourself—
every chance you get.
It will clear your vision
and free your soul.

TRANSIENCE

Death is a beautiful thing.
It is life and spirit
moving on like a butterfly.
What happens after this metamorphosis?
Your beauty was here
and now dances in my heart.
I'm glad you touched my life—
your love flutters all around me.

WABI SABI HEART

Whenever your heart breaks,
you can put it back together
in a more beautiful way.
The cracks can be filled with golden light
that brings back life and love.
Don't give up on your heart,
when it feels like it twinges with pain,
when it loses its beat,
or when it is lost in grief.
Take time
to lovingly care for your heart—
make love with your life.
This is the art of living.

THE I IN EVERY STORM

Sometimes you just gotta go through it—
the pain, the healing, the growth,
the resistance, the discomfort, the emotions,
the struggle.

You can do it in any way, shape, or form.
It can be graceful. It can be sloppy. It can be
fun. It can be difficult. It can be frustrating.

But choose to go through it and not around it.
What you want to avoid will always be there,
so why not surrender and face it head-on?
Let come whatever wants to come.
Will there ever be a better time?

Most things in life take courage,
and you are given all the courage
you need to overcome your battles.
You don't get to choose when it ends
or how it ends,
but you get to choose how you use your life
and who you will be.

muriel okubo

There are things in life
you have been through
or are going through
that will challenge you.

It is easy to give up
but when you go through it,
you know you did it without
forsaking yourself.

Just go through it.
Feel the emotions,
feel the resistance,
but keep going.
There is always an "I" in every storm—
the "I" that survives it all.
When you can be straight,
then you can cut through
the bullshit that isn't you
and emerge on the other side.
Stay true to your centre.
You got this.

free your soul

YOU ARE YOU

Every moment of every day,
is an opportunity to
shed the conditioning,
shed the programming,
shed the negative experiences,
shed the words that wounded you,
shed the beliefs that sought to destroy you
and, in this shedding,
you are pure,
you are love,
you are hope,
you are a gift,
you are a blessing,
you are renewed,
You are you.

WISDOM

When you choose growth,
you often choose discomfort—
taking space in new territory.
It can feel foreign and strange.
When the world feels heavy
and challenging,
come back to your heart.
This is where wisdom will give you rest.
It will beat for you
as you catch your breath.
Let the wisdom from your heart
fire your growth
and flow into everything you do.
A heart of love will never lead you wrong.

OPEN HEART

We will face trials on this earth.
We all come here with lessons to learn.
We will have seasons of pain, sorrow, and joy.
We can't predict with certainty
what lies ahead,
but our consciousness can continually grow.
When we are struggling,
let's take a moment
and see whether our hearts are open or closed.
An open heart allows for possibilities,
inspiration, and a new path.
A closed heart will see no way
and only the limitations.
Whether we want that relationship,
that healing,
that friendship,
that new career,
to repair that relationship
or that next adventure . . .

Everything starts and continues
with an open heart.
Let's be open to listening to our hearts
when we are in a frequency

muriel okubo

of clarity, truth, peace, and love.
A loving and open heart
will give us the wisdom and discernment
to know what fits,
and resonates
with our soul.

FORGIVENESS

We all walk around with different
consciousnesses—
every single person you meet has been through
something or is going through something.
We all have a past and a history.
Some of us have deeper wounds than others.
Some of us have more difficulty
letting go of our pains.
Some of us hurt others because of our hurts.
Some of us get hurt because
we are on the pathway of a storm.
Every time we face an injustice,
the only way we can move forward
is to forgive.
Life requires a whole lot of forgiving.
And it's true.
That person who broke our hearts.
That person who said the rudest thing ever.
That time they said one thing
and did the opposite.
That time they didn't show up for us.
That time they let us down.
That time we witnessed corruption.
That time they stole from us.

That time they left us.
That time they manipulated us.
That time we hurt ourselves.
That time when we could have done better.
There will never be a shortage of these times
as long as we all live
in different consciousnesses.
The best we can do
is forgive
again and again.
Forgive them.
Forgive ourselves.
Forgive the past.
Learn to release and understand
the experiences that arise from
a limited consciousness.
This is the energy of forgiveness.
We are here for giving
in the richness
of who we are.
We can bring grace
and growth to all things—
surrendering to all of it.
Let's let love flow again
from our hearts,
while we free our souls.

HOME

Where your heart
meets your soul.

THIS LIFE

What if you had to return
to this life all over again?
What are the soul lessons
you would have to repeat?
What if you could
use your remaining time on earth
to embody the lessons you have learned?
What would you change?
The gift is yours,
not sometime later,
but right now.

FREEDOM IN SURRENDER

I wish for you to look
at the parts that aren't pleasing to you—
the parts you are hiding,
not wanting to witness.
The parts that make you feel uncomfortable,
and powerless—
calling and needing exploration.
Exposed to the light,
you can care for them,
listen to them,
and give them the presence they call for—
please provide them
with the space they need
to unravel and be heard.
These parts of you
aren't to be feared or ashamed.
There is nothing you need to hide
but something you need to see.
Uncovering and dislodging
falsities you carry
will free you from a prison
with an unlocked door.
You will be free to sit with the truth

as you give light and witness
to all you hold so heavily.
Sometimes, the truth is dark,
but you can free yourself with light.
With your support,
darkness can be released and transformed,
giving you peace from what burdens you.
Your soul will call you to do the work.
Surrender to your freedom.

free your soul

WHOLENESS

When we approach life
from our wholeness,
instead of our woundedness,
we can let go of the expectations
we have of others.
We will discover what we need
from ourselves to restore peace
as we welcome the one in us.

muriel okubo

DIRECTIONS

The experience of love and truth,
never hurts—
it is our distance from them
that causes us to suffer.
Everything that pains us,
is an opportunity to bridge us
back to love.
Life is a compass showing us the
the direction of truth.

ALL YOU

Your trauma
was a weight you carried with you.
You kept it close,
believing you had to keep it
in the deep crevices of your heart.
You made it a story,
and you tucked it safely inside you.
You thought you had to protect
and comfort it,
then one day,
happiness knocked on your door.
You thought about it
and giving up this opportunity
that lovingly looked at you.
Right then and there,
you removed the bandage on your heart
and discovered there was nothing there.
The bandage was dirty and dusty
because you had kept it there,
believing you had something to hide,
to be ashamed of,
an ugliness to cover.
Oh, my heart,
underneath that,

muriel okubo

you were so beautiful.
You had no scar—
you were whole.
You tried to hide yourself from yourself.
When did you become so beautiful?
You need not blind yourself again
and run back inside.
You will grab happiness by the hand
and never let it go.
You will kiss it on the lips,
embrace it with your being,
open and exposed.
You let it lead you
to much more—
more laughter,
more love,
more pinch-me moments.
This is where your heart beats,
this is where your heart belongs.

free your soul

RETURNING TO SOURCE

You have known darkness,
you have known loneliness,
you have known sadness,
you have known anger,
you have known fear,
but, today,
you know your light,
you know your wholeness,
you know your joy,
you know your peace,
you know your love
and, most of all,
you know that today is a choice
to release the past
because it is not where you will stay.
You are blessed to have experienced it all,
but today you can choose your present.
You were made to dance in your divinity,
and it shows you who you are.
you are light,
you are whole,
you are joy,
you are peace,
you are love.

muriel okubo

WORTHY

The greatest investment is
the one you make in yourself.
The effort,
the strength,
the sweat,
the tears,
the patience,
the resistance,
the love,
because, in the end,
what you put into yourself
can never be taken away.
The integrity of your being
is in every fibre of you.
What you do with your life
holds great meaning—
there is no such thing as failure.
You are worthy of all good things
even when it looks like the opposite.
Please remember this,
the next time,
when you doubt your ability to receive.

free your soul

TRUTH BE TOLD

Unapologetically,
being yourself
takes practice.
It takes a willingness to see who you are,
to see who you have become
and face the one living inside—
the one who is scared,
the one who is unsure,
the one who is insecure,
the one who doesn't want to change.
And when you step away
from these patterns and programs,
you begin to notice
a breaking down of everything
you have known—
the one who wants to break free,
the one who is confident,
the one who is certain,
the one who is secure,
the one who wants change.
In this journey of accepting life
as a process of letting go,
and surrendering to the truth,

you realize the old ways prevent
new blessings from reaching you
but in transformation anchored in truth,
you discover you are free
to be everything you were meant to be.

free your soul

RESTORATION

When you listen to someone's soul
and remind them of who they are,
you restore the flow of love
in them,
between you,
and in you.

PURPOSE

Sweet soul,
this is a reminder that your life
has no limits.
You have been blessed with gifts
the world needs.
Please share them
and let others be blessed by them, too.
You are here for a reason
and that reason
is to shine.

GOLDEN LIGHT

There is great beauty that dwells within,
an energy that lives in each of us,
that juiciness and wholeness of Source.
It is in the soft, fleshy face of a child
captured by a story,
in the unmarked surf blue sky,
in the stars glowing a brilliant, jewelled map
in the darkest night.
It's in the life force in my hands creating
form with clay on a pottery wheel.
It's in my mother's eyes
and everything she comforts or embraces.

It is a true gift to touch something
and leave it changed forever.
This is the beauty of life.
This is the beauty of creation.

TRUTH

The fullness of who you are
is beautiful.
The practice of life will allow
you to discover this for yourself—
by releasing stories,
being open to inspiration,
and putting your whole heart
into what moves you.
Come back to the truth
when life gets tough,
and it will guide you
with grace and confidence.
This conscious practice is your task
until the end of your days.

ONENESS

Sometimes, all it takes is one.
One person,
one conversation,
one smile,
one powerful experience,
one witness,
one book,
one chance,
one heart,
one life,
one truth,
one opportunity,
one decision,
one step,
one change,
one voice,
one movie,
one story,
one challenge,
one flame,
one death,
one love,
one heartbreak,
one loss,

muriel okubo

one trip,
one success,
one kiss,
one message,
one kindness,
one stand.

Sometimes, all it takes is one
to be better than you were,
to open your heart again,
to show you what love truly is,
to align to the truth of who you are,
to reveal your desires,
to propel you into your destiny,
to love yourself with compassion,
to honour your needs,
to let go,
to discover the truth,
to help fulfill your purpose,
to change your life forever,
to heal a wound,
to save a life,
to save a soul,
to save your life,
to save your soul,
to save humanity.

THANK YOU FOR PURCHASING 'FREE YOUR SOUL'

Sharing poetry from my heart is one way that my soul speaks. Creating this book has been a labour of love into which I poured my heart. I hope you found this collection of prose and poetry inspiring and meaningful.

If you've found 'Free Your Soul' to be a source of inspiration, I would love it if you shared your thoughts in a review. Your feedback is invaluable to me. Thank you once again!

Warmly,

Muriel Okubo

ABOUT THE AUTHOR

Muriel Okubo is a Canadian-Japanese author, artist, and Doctor of Traditional Asian Medicine. She has had a busy practice for over sixteen years in which she has treated people from all walks of life and all ages struggling with various issues. Having witnessed the pains of the human condition and the beauty of the human spirit, she wishes to inspire and encourage everyone on their path.

Understanding that body-mind-spirit health is crucial for wellness, she has created beautiful books to help people integrate their physical, mental, emotional, and spiritual bodies. She has always loved the power of writing as a connection to her heart and soul. Muriel is passionate about sharing the ideas and practices that have helped her the most on her path to living more consciously. She desires that everyone follow their inner wisdom and find the truth of their soul.

Subscribe to my Newsletter

www.ingramcontent.com/pod-product-compliance
Lightning Source LLC
Chambersburg PA
CBHW020735020526
44118CB00033B/720